Piano Play-Along

FRANK SINATRA
MOST REQUESTED SONGS

Cover photo courtesy of Photofest

ISBN-13: 978-1-4234-0500-9
ISBN-10: 1-4234-0500-5

HAL•LEONARD®
CORPORATION
7777 W. BLUEMOUND RD. P.O. BOX 13819 MILWAUKEE, WI 53213

Visit Hal Leonard Online at
www.halleonard.com

CONTENTS

ALL THE WAY

Words by SAMMY CAHN
Music by JAMES VAN HEUSEN

When some-bod-y loves you, it's no good un-less he loves you all the
When some-bod-y needs you, it's no good un-less she needs you all the

way.
way.

Hap-py to be near you, when you need some-one to cheer you
Thru the good or lean years and for all the in-be-tween years,

all the way.
come what may.

Tall-er _____ than the tall-est tree is,
Who knows _____ where the road will lead us,

THE BIRTH OF THE BLUES

Words by B.G. DeSYLVA and LEW BROWN
Music by RAY HENDERSON

They say some peo-ple long a-go were search-ing for a diff-'rent

Oh!

FROM HERE TO ETERNITY

Words by ROBERT WELLS
Music by FRED KARGER

I'VE GOT THE WORLD ON A STRING

Lyric by TED KOEHLER
Music by HAROLD ARLEN

Mer - ry month of May, sun - ny

WITCHCRAFT

Lyric by CAROLYN LEIGH
Music by CY COLEMAN

THEME FROM "NEW YORK, NEW YORK"

Words by FRED EBB
Music by JOHN KANDER

king of the hill, _____ top of the heap.

My lit - tle town blues are melt - ing a -

way. I'll make a brand - new start ___ of it

in old New York. If I can

NIGHT AND DAY

Words and Music by
COLE PORTER

Like the beat, beat, beat of the tom - tom; when the jun - gle shad - ows

fall, like the tick, tick, tock of the state - ly clock, as it stands a - gainst the

wall, like the drip, drip, drip of the rain - drops, when the sum - mer show'r is

TIME AFTER TIME

Words by SAMMY CAHN
Music by JULE STYNE

What good are words I say to you? They can't con-vey to you what's in my heart. If you could hear

THE ULTIMATE SONGBOOKS

These great songbook/CD packs come with our standard arrangements for piano and voice with guitar chord frames plus a CD. The CD includes a full performance of each song, as well as a second track without the piano part so you can play "lead" with the band!

Vol. 1 Movie Music
Come What May • Forrest Gump – Main Title (Feather Theme) • My Heart Will Go On (Love Theme from Titanic) • The Rainbow Connection • Tears in Heaven • A Time for Us • Up Where We Belong • Where Do I Begin (Love Theme).
00311072 P/V/G........................$12.95

Vol. 2 Jazz Ballads
Autumn in New York • Do You Know What It Means to Miss New Orleans • Georgia on My Mind • In a Sentimental Mood • More Than You Know • The Nearness of You • The Very Thought of You • When Sunny Gets Blue.
00311073 P/V/G........................$12.95

Vol. 3 Timeless Pop
Ebony and Ivory • Every Breath You Take • From a Distance • I Write the Songs • In My Room • Let It Be • Oh, Pretty Woman • We've Only Just Begun.
00311074 P/V/G........................$12.95

Vol. 4 Broadway Classics
Ain't Misbehavin' • Cabaret • If I Were a Bell • Memory • Oklahoma • Some Enchanted Evening • The Sound of Music • You'll Never Walk Alone.
00311075 P/V/G........................$12.95

Vol. 5 Disney
Beauty and the Beast • Can You Feel the Love Tonight • Colors of the Wind • Go the Distance • Look Through My Eyes • A Whole New World • You'll Be in My Heart • You've Got a Friend in Me.
00311076 P/V/G........................$12.95

Vol. 6 Country Standards
Blue Eyes Crying in the Rain • Crazy • King of the Road • Oh, Lonesome Me • Ring of Fire • Tennessee Waltz • You Are My Sunshine • Your Cheatin' Heart.
00311077 P/V/G........................$12.95

Vol. 7 Love Songs
Can't Help Falling in Love • (They Long to Be) Close to You • Here, There and Everywhere • How Deep Is Your Love • I Honestly Love You • Maybe I'm Amazed • Wonderful Tonight • You Are So Beautiful.
00311078 P/V/G........................$12.95

Vol. 8 Classical Themes
Can Can • Habanera • Humoresque • In the Hall of the Mountain King • Minuet in G Major • Piano Concerto No. 21 in C Major, 2nd Movement Excerpt • Prelude in E Minor, Op. 28, No. 4 • Symphony No. 5 in C Minor, 1st Movement Excerpt.
00311079 Piano Solo $12.95

Vol. 9 Children's Songs
Do-Re-Mi • It's a Small World • Linus and Lucy • Sesame Street Theme • Sing • Winnie the Pooh • Won't You Be My Neighbor? • Yellow Submarine.
0311080 P/V/G $12.95

Vol. 10 Wedding Classics
Air on the G String • Ave Maria • Bridal Chorus • Canon in D • Jesu, Joy of Man's Desiring • Ode to Joy • Trumpet Voluntary • Wedding March.
00311081 Piano Solo.................$12.95

Vol. 11 Wedding Favorites
All I Ask of You • Don't Know Much • Endless Love • Grow Old with Me • In My Life • Longer • Wedding Processional • You and I.
00311097 P/V/G $12.95

Vol. 12 Christmas Favorites
Blue Christmas • The Christmas Song • Do You Hear What I Hear • Here Comes Santa Claus • I Saw Mommy Kissing Santa Claus • Let It Snow! Let It Snow! Let It Snow! • Merry Christmas, Darling • Silver Bells.
00311137 P/V/G $12.95

Vol. 13 Yuletide Favorites
Angels We Have Heard on High • Away in a Manger • Deck the Hall • The First Noel • Go, Tell It on the Mountain • Jingle Bells • Joy to the World • O Little Town of Bethlehem.
00311138 P/V/G........................$12.95

Vol. 14 Pop Ballads
Have I Told You Lately • I'll Be There for You • It's All Coming Back to Me Now • Looks Like We Made It • Rainy Days and Monday • Say You, Say Me • She's Got a Way • Your Song.
00311145 P/V/G........................$12.95

Vol. 15 Favorite Standards
Call Me • The Girl from Ipanema • Moon River • My Way • Satin Doll • Smoke Gets in Your Eyes • Strangers in the Night • The Way You Look Tonight.
00311146 P/V/G........................$12.95

Vol. 16 TV Classics
The Brady Bunch • Green Acres Theme • Happy Days • Johnny's Theme • Love Boat Theme • Mister Ed • The Munsters Theme • Where Everybody Knows Your Name.
00311147 P/V/G........................$12.95

Vol. 17 Movie Favorites
Back to the Future • Theme from E.T. • Footloose • For All We Know • Somewhere in Time • Somewhere Out There • Theme from Terms of Endearment • You Light Up My Life.
00311148 P/V/G........................$12.95

Vol. 18 Jazz Standards
All the Things You Are • Bluesette • Easy Living • I'll Remember April • Isn't It Romantic? • Stella by Starlight • Tangerine • Yesterdays.
00311149 P/V/G........................$12.95

Vol. 19 Contemporary Hits
Beautiful • Calling All Angels • Don't Know Why • If I Ain't Got You • 100 Years • This Love • A Thousand Miles • You Raise Me Up.
00311162 P/V/G........................$12.95

Vol. 20 R&B Ballads
After the Love Has Gone • All in Love Is Fair • Hello • I'll Be There • Let's Stay Together • Midnight Train to Georgia • Tell It like It Is • Three Times a Lady.
00311163 P/V/G........................$12.95

Vol. 21 Big Band
All or Nothing at All • Apple Honey • April in Paris • Cherokee • In the Mood • Opus One • Stardust • Stompin' at the Savoy.
00311164 P/V/G........................$12.95

Vol. 22 Rock Classics
Against All Odds • Bennie and the Jets • Come Sail Away • Do It Again • Free Bird • Jump • Wanted Dead or Alive • We Are the Champions.
00311165 P/V/G........................$12.95

Vol. 23 Worship Classics
Awesome God • How Majestic Is Your Name • Lord, Be Glorified • Lord, I Lift Your Name on High • Praise the Name of Jesus • Shine, Jesus, Shine • Step by Step • There Is a Redeemer.
00311166 P/V/G........................$12.95

Vol. 24 Les Misérables
Bring Him Home • Castle on a Cloud • Do You Hear the People Sing? • Drink with Me • Empty Chairs at Empty Tables • I Dreamed a Dream • A Little Fall of Rain • On My Own.
00311169 P/V/G........................$14.95

Vol. 25 The Sound of Music
Climb Ev'ry Mountain • Do-Re-Mi • Edelweiss • Maria • My Favorite Things • Sixteen Going on Seventeen • Something Good • The Sound of Music.
00311175 P/V/G........................$14.95

Vol. 26 Andrew Lloyd Webber Favorites
All I Ask of You • Amigos Para Siempre • As If We Never Said Goodbye • Everything's Alright • Memory • No Matter What • Tell Me on a Sunday • You Must Love Me.
00311178 P/V/G........................$12.95

Vol. 27 Andrew Lloyd Webber Greats
Any Dream Will Do • Don't Cry for Me Argentina • I Don't Know How to Love Him • The Music of the Night • The Phantom of the Opera • Unexpected Song • Whistle Down the Wind • With One Look.
00311179 P/V/G........................$12.95

Vol. 28 Lennon & McCartney
Eleanor Rigby • Hey Jude • The Long and Winding Road • Love Me Do • Lucy in the Sky with Diamonds • Nowhere Man • Strawberry Fields Forever • Yesterday.
00311180 P/V/G........................$12.95

Vol. 29 The Beach Boys
Barbara Ann • Be True to Your School • California Girls • Fun, Fun, Fun • Help Me Rhonda • I Get Around • Little Deuce Coupe • Wouldn't It Be Nice.
00311181 P/V/G........................$12.95

Vol. 30 Elton John
Candle in the Wind • Crocodile Rock • Daniel • Goodbye Yellow Brick Road • I Guess That's Why They Call It the Blues • Levon • Sorry Seems to Be the Hardest Word • Your Song.
00311182 P/V/G........................$12.95

Vol. 31 Carpenters
(They Long to Be) Close to You • For All We Know • I Won't Last a Day without You • Only Yesterday • Rainy Days and Mondays • Top of the World • We've Only Just Begun • Yesterday Once More.
00311183 P/V/G........................$12.95

Vol. 32 Bacharach & David
Alfie • Close to You • Do You Know the Way to San Jose • A House Is Not a Home • The Look of Love • Raindrops Keep Fallin' on My Head • What the World Needs Now Is Love • Wives and Lovers.
00311218 P/V/G........................$12.95

Vol. 33 Peanuts™
Blue Charlie Brown • Charlie Brown Theme • The Great Pumpkin Waltz • Joe Cool • Linus and Lucy • Oh, Good Grief • Red Baron • You're in Love, Charlie Brown.
00311227 P/V/G........................$12.95

Vol. 34 Charlie Brown Christmas
Christmas Is Coming • The Christmas Song • Christmas Time Is Here • Linus and Lucy • My Little Drum • O Tannenbaum • Skating • What Child Is This.
00311228 P/V/G........................$12.95

Vol. 35 Elvis Presley Hits
Blue Suede Shoes • Can't Help Falling in Love • Don't Be Cruel (To a Heart That's True) • Heartbreak Hotel • I Want You, I Need You, I Love You • It's Now or Never • Love Me • (Let Me Be Your) Teddy Bear.
00311230 P/V/G........................$12.95

Vol. 36 Elvis Presley Greats
All Shook Up • Don't • Jailhouse Rock • Love Me Tender • Loving You • Return to Sender • Too Much • Wooden Heart.
00311231 P/V/G........................$12.95

Vol. 37 Contemporary Christian
El Shaddai • Every Season • Here I Am • Jesus Will Still Be There • Let Us Pray • Place in This World • Who Am I • Wisdom.
00311232 P/V/G........................$12.95

Vol. 38 Duke Ellington – Standards
Caravan • Do Nothin' Till You Hear from Me • I Got It Bad and That Ain't Good • In a Sentimental Mood • It Don't Mean a Thing (If It Ain't Got That Swing) • Love You Madly • Mood Indigo • Sophisticated Lady.
00311233 P/V/G $14.95

Vol. 39 Duke Ellington – Classics
Come Sunday • Don't Get Around Much Anymore • I Let a Song Go out of My Heart • I'm Beginning to See the Light • In a Mellow Tone • Satin Doll • Solitude • Take the "A" Train.
00311234 P/V/G........................$14.95

Vol. 40 Showtunes
The Best of Times • Hello, Dolly! • I'll Know • Mame • Summer Nights • Till There Was You • Tomorrow • What I Did for Love.
00311237 P/V/G........................$12.95

Vol. 41 Rodgers & Hammerstein
Bali Ha'i • Do I Love You Because You're Beautiful? • Hello, Young Lovers • If I Loved You • It Might As Well Be Spring • Love, Look Away • Oh, What a Beautiful Mornin' • The Sweetest Sounds.
00311238 P/V/G........................$12.95

Vol. 42 Irving Berlin
Always • Blue Skies • Change Partners • Cheek to Cheek • Easter Parade • How Deep Is the Ocean (How High Is the Sky) • Puttin' on the Ritz • What'll I Do?
00311239 P/V/G........................$14.95

Vol. 43 Jerome Kern
Can't Help Lovin' Dat Man • A Fine Romance • The Folks Who Live on the Hill • I Won't Dance • I'm Old Fashioned • The Last Time I Saw Paris • Long Ago (And Far Away) • Ol' Man River.
00311240 P/V/G........................$14.95

Vol. 44 Frank Sinatra – Popular Hits
Come Fly with Me • Cycles • High Hopes • Love and Marriage • My Way • Strangers in the Night • (Love Is) The Tender Trap • Young at Heart.
00311277 P/V/G........................$14.95

Vol. 45 Frank Sinatra – Most Requested Songs
All the Way • The Birth of the Blues • From Here to Eternity • I've Got the World on a String • Theme from "New York, New York" • Night and Day • Time After Time • Witchcraft.
00311278 P/V/G........................$14.95

Vol. 46 Wicked
Dancing Through Life • Defying Gravity • For Good • I Couldn't Be Happier • I'm Not That Girl • Popular • What Is This Feeling? • The Wizard and I.
00311317 P/V/G........................$12.95

Vol. 47 Rent
I'll Cover You • Light My Candle • One Song Glory • Out Tonight • Rent • Seasons of Love • What You Own • Without You.
00311319 P/V/G........................$12.95

Vol. 48 Christmas Carols
God Rest Ye Merry, Gentlemen • Hark! The Herald Angels Sing • It Came upon the Midnight Clear • O Come, All Ye Faithful (Adeste Fideles) • O Holy Night • Silent Night • We Three Kings of Orient Are • What Child Is This?
00311332 P/V/G........................$12.95

Vol. 49 Holiday Hits
Frosty the Snow Man • Happy Xmas (War Is Over) • (There's No Place Like) Home for the Holidays • I'll Be Home for Christmas • Jingle-Bell Rock • Rockin' Around the Christmas Tree • Rudolph the Red-Nosed Reindeer • Santa Claus Is Comin' to Town.
00311333 P/V/G........................$12.95

FOR MORE INFORMATION, SEE YOUR LOCAL MUSIC DEALER, OR WRITE TO:

HAL•LEONARD® CORPORATION

7777 W. BLUEMOUND RD. P.O. BOX 13819 MILWAUKEE, WI 53213

Visit Hal Leonard Online at **www.halleonard.com**

Prices, contents and availability subject to change without notice.

1206